The Impact of NLP Techniques on Improving Time Management Skills

By Rex Morton

The Impact of NLP Techniques on Improving Time Management Skills

Disclaimer

This book is intended to provide information about the fields of Neuro-Linguistic Programming (NLP) and Cognitive Behavioural Therapy (CBT) and their potential integration. While the author has made every effort to ensure that the information was correct at the time of publication, the author does not assume and hereby disclaims any liability to any party for any loss, damage, or disruption caused by errors or omissions, whether such errors or omissions result from negligence, accident, or any other cause.

The contents of this book should not be used as a substitute for professional advice, diagnosis, or treatment. The reader should always consult with a qualified healthcare provider about any mental health concerns or conditions. Never disregard professional psychological or medical advice or delay in seeking it because of something you have read in this book.

The views expressed in this work are solely those of the author and do not necessarily reflect the views of the publisher, and the publisher hereby disclaims any responsibility for them.

The inclusion of websites, links, or references to other resources does not mean that the author or the publisher endorses the information the organization or website may provide or recommendations it might make. Furthermore, the author does not guarantee the accuracy of the information these resources provide.

The use of any information provided in this book is solely at your own risk.

The study of the human mind has always been a complex and fascinating endeavor. Over the centuries, many theories and techniques have emerged, attempting to decipher the intricate webs of our thought processes and behavior patterns. Among these, Neuro-Linguistic Programming (NLP) has made significant strides since its conception in the 1970s.

NLP, a psychological strategy developed by Richard Bandler and John Grinder, includes examining the tactics employed by successful people and using them to accomplish one's own objectives. It links ideas, words, and behavioural patterns acquired via experience to certain results. NLP proponents say that each of us creates a unique worldview and lives according to it, which shapes our attitudes, conduct, and decisions.

On the other hand, the modern world is built around the concept of time, with nearly every aspect of our lives being governed by the clock and calendar. The way we manage our time can significantly impact our productivity, effectiveness, and overall quality of life. Effective time management allows us to accomplish more in a shorter period, reducing stress and enabling us to focus on activities that align with our goals.

This book, "The Impact of Neuro-Linguistic Programming Techniques on Improving Time Management Skills", explores the intersection of NLP and time management. It delves into how the techniques and principles of NLP can be applied to enhance our time management skills, helping us become more productive, effective, and balanced in our personal and professional lives. It provides insights into the theory and practical applications of NLP, the psychology of time management, and the synergy of the two to lead a more fulfilled life.

Before we embark on this journey, let's familiarize ourselves with some key terms and definitions:

Neuro-Linguistic Programming (NLP): A psychological approach that combines insights from cognitive and neurological science, linguistics, and psychology to understand human behavior and modify it to achieve desired outcomes.

Time management: Is the process of organizing and planning how to split your day up between different tasks in order to be more productive and efficient.

Goal Setting: The establishment of objectives that a person or organization hopes to achieve over a certain period.

Prioritization: The action or process of deciding the importance or urgency of tasks and allocating time and resources accordingly.

Procrastination: The act of delaying or postponing tasks or actions to a later time, often leading to stress, poor performance, and a feeling of guilt.

Stress Management: Techniques and strategies to cope with or lessen the physical and emotional effects of everyday life pressure.

Work-Life Balance: The harmony between professional obligations and extracurricular pursuits, promoting wellbeing.

As we progress through each chapter, we will delve deeper into these concepts, unraveling the potential of NLP in reshaping our time management abilities. Whether you are a seasoned professional, a student, or anyone aiming to maximize your time and productivity, this book aims to provide a fresh perspective and practical tools to make the most of your time.

Neuro-Linguistic Programming (NLP) is a compelling and revolutionary approach to communication, personal development, and psychotherapy that has been utilized and studied since the 1970s. Its rich history and underlying principles make it a fascinating area of study for anyone interested in understanding human behavior and leveraging it to create meaningful changes in their lives.

Origins and Development of NLP

NLP was conceived in the mid-1970s by Richard Bandler, a student of psychology, and John Grinder, a professor of linguistics, at the University of California, Santa Cruz. Their initial goal was to model the therapeutic skills of Fritz Perls (the founder of Gestalt therapy), Virginia Satir (the founder of Family Systems Therapy), and later, Milton H. Erickson (a pioneering hypnotherapist).

They sought to uncover why these individuals were exceptionally successful in their field and if their methods could be replicated. Through their research, Bandler and Grinder established a set of tools, techniques, and communication ideas that became the groundwork of NLP.

Over the decades, NLP has grown, evolved, and been subject to both praise and criticism. Today, it is used in various fields, including business, coaching, therapy, and personal development, to improve communication, motivation, and behavioral patterns.

Core Principles and Presuppositions of NLP

NLP is founded on several principles or presuppositions, which are beliefs or guiding principles that NLP practitioners adopt to create a conducive environment for change and learning. Here are some of the core principles:

The Map is not the Territory: Our perceptions of reality are subjective and do not reflect the reality itself but our 'map' or interpretation of it.

Experience has Structure: Our thoughts and behaviors follow patterns. By understanding and altering these patterns, we can change our behaviors and thoughts.

If one person can do something, anyone can learn to do it: NLP posits that any human ability can be modeled and taught to others.

The Mind and Body are part of the same system: Our thoughts, emotions, body, and actions are interconnected and influence one another.

There is no failure, only feedback: Any outcome is a form of feedback. Rather than viewing it as failure, we should use it to adapt and improve.

Techniques and Models of NLP

Several techniques and models have been developed within NLP. Here are some key examples:

The Meta-Model: A model for asking questions and gathering information that challenges and expands a person's mental maps, thus enabling them to think more clearly and broadly.

The Milton-Model: A method of using vague and metaphorical language to induce trance and facilitate change, inspired by Milton H. Erickson's therapeutic techniques.

Anchoring: A method of connecting an internal reaction to an external or internal trigger so that the reaction can be rapidly and occasionally quietly retrieved again.

Swish Patterns: A technique for changing behaviors by diverting a mental pattern that leads to an undesired behavior to one that leads to a desired behavior.

Visual/Kinesthetic Disassociation (VKD): A method for reducing the impact of negative memories or phobias.

Understanding these fundamentals of NLP provides a firm foundation to delve into its application in improving our time management skills, which we will explore in subsequent chapters. The power of NLP lies not just in its techniques but also in understanding its principles and adopting an open, curious, and flexible mindset.

Time management is a critical skill in our increasingly fast-paced world. It involves the way we organize, allocate, and plan our time to efficiently execute specific activities. Understanding time, its psychological aspects, and the implications of effective time management are integral to our personal and professional success.

Defining Time Management

Time management is the process of organizing and planning how to distribute your time between specific tasks to increase efficiency and productivity. It is a skill that enables us to control our time effectively, ensuring we get the most out of it. Good time management requires an element of planning, prioritizing tasks according to their importance or urgency, and the discipline to follow through on those plans.

The Psychological Aspects of Time

The way we perceive time can have a significant impact on how we manage it. Our perception of time is influenced by our mood, attention, and the nature of our tasks. For instance, when we are deeply engrossed in an activity or enjoying what we are doing, time seems to 'fly.' Conversely, when we are bored or anxious, time appears to 'drag.'

Furthermore, our tendency to underestimate how long tasks will take – a phenomenon known as the planning fallacy – can often lead to poor time management. Overcoming these psychological barriers requires us to be aware of them and employ strategies to minimize their impact.

The Consequences of Poor Time Management

Poor time management can have various negative effects. At a personal level, it can lead to stress, burnout, and a sense of being overwhelmed. It can also result in poor work performance, missed deadlines, and increased pressure.

Moreover, consistently poor time management can have long-term consequences, including damaged personal and professional relationships, decreased opportunities for growth, and a diminished quality of life. These effects highlight the importance of learning to manage time effectively.

The Benefits of Effective Time Management

Effective time management, on the other hand, has numerous benefits. It increases productivity and efficiency, allowing us to achieve more with less effort. It provides better control over our tasks, reducing feelings of stress and overwhelm.

Good time management also allows for better decision-making since it ensures that adequate time is allocated for contemplation and assessment. It promotes work-life balance, ensuring that we have time for our personal interests and hobbies outside of work.

Moreover, effective time management can lead to improved career prospects. Those who consistently meet deadlines and manage their workload effectively are more likely to be recognized and rewarded in the workplace.

In conclusion, understanding time management's importance and the implications of doing it effectively are key steps to improving our time management skills. In the upcoming chapters, we will delve into the ways Neuro-Linguistic Programming can help us harness the power of time more effectively.

While the importance of good time management cannot be overstated, effectively implementing it can be challenging. Neuro-Linguistic Programming, with its focus on understanding and influencing brain behavior, provides a unique approach to improve time management skills.

Understanding the Correlation Between the Brain, Behavior, and Time Management

Our perception of time and our behavior towards it is largely dictated by our brain's functioning. For instance, our brains are naturally prone to favor immediate rewards over delayed ones, a cognitive bias known as temporal discounting. This bias can often lead us to procrastinate, preferring tasks that provide immediate gratification and postponing those that contribute to long-term benefits.

Our brains also tend to underestimate the time required to complete tasks, a phenomenon known as the planning fallacy, leading to inefficient time management. Besides, habitual behaviors, engrained in our neural pathways, can also influence our approach to managing time, sometimes creating unproductive routines.

How NLP can Impact Perception and Utilization of Time

NLP offers a powerful set of tools and techniques to address the cognitive and behavioral challenges associated with time management. Here's how:

Reframing Perceptions: Through techniques such as reframing, NLP allows us to change our perception of time. We can replace unhelpful views, such as seeing time as a scarce resource, with more empowering ones, such as seeing time as abundant and well within our control.

Overcoming Procrastination: NLP techniques like future pacing and visualization can help overcome procrastination. By creating a compelling vision of the future benefits of completing a task, our brains can be nudged to favor long-term rewards over short-term gratification.

Improving Planning: NLP can also address the planning fallacy. Techniques such as timeline therapy can help individuals develop a more realistic sense of time, improving their ability to plan and allocate time to tasks.

Changing Habits: With NLP, we can also change habitual behaviors that contribute to poor time management. Techniques such as anchoring and the Swish pattern can help in forming productive habits and breaking unproductive ones.

By understanding the interplay between NLP and time management, we can utilize NLP's techniques to transform our perception of time and our behaviors related to it. In the following chapters, we will delve deeper into specific NLP techniques and their application to time management, providing practical insights to revolutionize your approach to managing your time.

Our perception of time can greatly impact how we manage it. By modifying our time perceptions using NLP techniques, we can better control how we interact with time, leading to improved time management.

Techniques for Modifying Perceptions of Time

Time Distortion: This technique allows you to experience time differently. For instance, if a task feels like it's dragging on, you can use time distortion to make it feel as though it's going by more quickly. This technique involves visualization and self-suggestion - imagining the task passing more swiftly and telling yourself that time is passing quickly.

Timeline Therapy: This technique involves visualizing your 'timeline' - how you mentally represent the past, present, and future. By manipulating this mental timeline, you can change your perception of time. For instance, if you perceive a future task as too distant to start working on it, you can bring it closer on your mental timeline to foster urgency and motivation.

The Application of Anchoring, Reframing, and Other NLP Techniques to Manage Time Perception

Anchoring: Anchoring involves creating a trigger or 'anchor' for a specific mental state. For example, you might create an anchor for a state of focus and productivity. You can then activate this anchor when starting a task, helping you to get into the productive mindset more quickly.

Example: You could use the act of sitting down at your desk and opening your laptop as an anchor. Over time, this action will become associated with starting work and will help trigger a state of focus and productivity.

Reframing: Reframing involves changing the way you perceive a situation or experience. If you view a task as time-consuming and boring, you're likely to procrastinate on it. But if you can reframe it as a challenge or an opportunity to learn, you'll change your perception of the time it takes and might be more motivated to tackle it.

Example: Suppose you need to complete a lengthy report. Instead of viewing it as a boring task, reframe it as an opportunity to showcase your expertise and understanding of the subject. This shift in perception can make the task seem less daunting and the time required more acceptable.

Visual/Kinesthetic Disassociation (VKD): This technique can help to manage the stress or overwhelm associated with larger tasks that seem to require a lot of time. VKD involves mentally 'stepping out' of the situation and viewing it from an outsider's perspective. This can help to create emotional distance and provide a clearer view of the task.

Example: If a project feels overwhelming, close your eyes and visualize yourself completing the project. Imagine watching a movie of yourself efficiently managing your time, overcoming obstacles, and successfully finishing the project. This can make the project seem more manageable and less overwhelming.

By employing these NLP techniques, we can change our perception of time, allowing us to manage it more effectively. In the following chapters, we'll delve into how these techniques can be practically implemented for better time management in various life contexts.

Setting goals is a critical part of effective time management. However, it's not enough to merely set goals; they must be clear, attainable, and aligned with our overall objectives. By incorporating NLP techniques into goal setting, we can create robust, time-bound goals that guide our actions and optimize our time usage.

Defining SMART Goals in the NLP Context

SMART is an acronym that stands for Specific, Measurable, Achievable, Relevant, and Time-bound, all crucial qualities of a well-defined goal. In the context of NLP, these elements are amplified by our understanding of neurology and linguistics:

Specific: NLP encourages detailed visualization, which aligns with defining specific goals. The more specific the goal, the more easily our brain can visualize and work towards it.

Measurable: Goals need to have a criteria for success. In NLP, we use sensory-based description, describing what we'll see, hear, and feel when the goal is achieved.

Achievable: NLP stresses the belief that if someone else can achieve it, so can we. This aligns with setting goals that are challenging yet within reach.

Relevant: The goal should be in line with our broader objectives and values, a principle emphasized in NLP's outcome orientation.

Time-bound: A goal needs a deadline. NLP's timeline techniques can help us visualize the timeline and keep track of progress.

Using NLP Techniques for Setting and Achieving Time-Bound Goals

Well-Formed Outcome: This NLP technique ensures that your goal is positive, within your control, sensory-based, and ecological (i.e., considering the wider impacts of your goal). A well-formed outcome will also include a timeframe.

Example: Instead of setting a goal like "I want to stop wasting so much time", a well-formed outcome would be "By the end of the quarter, I will spend at least two focused hours each day on the project, which I'll track by keeping a daily log of my time."

Perceptual Positions: This NLP tool allows you to view your goals from different perspectives (first person, second person, and third person). This holistic perspective can ensure the goal is well-rounded and achievable.

Example: If your goal is to "Complete the project by the end of the month", you might consider how you (first person), your team members (second person), and an external observer (third person) would perceive this goal.

Visualization and the Future Pacing Technique

Visualization is a powerful NLP tool that can be used to embed your goals deeply into your unconscious mind. By vividly imagining achieving your goal, you create a clear direction for your mind to work towards.

Future pacing takes visualization a step further by asking you to project yourself into the future, to a point where you've already achieved your goal. It helps to solidify the goal in your mind and aids in creating a clear action plan.

Example: If your goal is to "Finish writing the book by the end of the year", visualize yourself holding the finished manuscript, feeling the sense of accomplishment, and celebrating your success. This mental rehearsal programs your mind to work towards making this vision a reality.

By integrating NLP techniques into goal setting, we can create more effective, time-bound goals that not only improve our time management but also increase our chances of success in achieving what we set out to do.

Effective time management also involves making good decisions and prioritizing tasks. Using NLP techniques, we can enhance our decision-making abilities and prioritize more effectively, further optimizing our time management.

Exploring NLP Techniques for Enhancing Decision-Making Capabilities

Meta-Modeling: This NLP technique involves asking precise questions to clarify information and understand situations more deeply. It's especially useful for decision-making as it can help clarify goals and uncover potential obstacles.

Example: If you're unsure whether to take on a new project, you might ask yourself: "What specifically will this project help me achieve? What challenges might arise? How will this impact my other commitments?"

The Disney Strategy: This technique involves adopting three different perspectives when making a decision - the Dreamer, the Realist, and the Critic. Each perspective serves a unique role in the decision-making process, allowing for a more comprehensive evaluation of your options.

Example: If you're deciding whether to start a new business, the Dreamer might visualize the best possible outcome, the Realist might consider the practical steps to achieve it, and the Critic might identify potential challenges and shortcomings.

Application of the NLP Techniques for Effective Prioritization

Chunking: This technique involves breaking down larger tasks into smaller, more manageable "chunks." By doing this, we can prioritize these smaller tasks more easily and make the larger task seem less overwhelming.

Example: If you have a large project due in a month, you might break it down into weekly and then daily tasks. This can help you prioritize these tasks more effectively and keep track of your progress.

Association/Dissociation: This NLP technique involves imagining a task from a deeply associated, first-person perspective and then from a dissociated, third-person perspective. This can help to evaluate a task's importance and urgency more effectively.

Example: If you're unsure about the importance of a task, first imagine performing it from a first-person perspective, then observe yourself performing it from a third-person perspective. This can help clarify the emotional importance and logical significance of the task, assisting in prioritization.

Outcome Specification: This involves clearly defining what you want to achieve from a task. By knowing what outcome you desire, you can prioritize tasks based on their relevance to your goals.

Example: If you're faced with several tasks, you might ask yourself: "What specifically do I want to achieve from each of these tasks? How do these tasks align with my broader goals?" The answers can help you prioritize the tasks.

Using NLP techniques can drastically enhance our decision-making and prioritization capabilities. By making better decisions and prioritizing tasks more effectively, we can improve our time management and increase our productivity and efficiency.

Procrastination, or the act of delaying or postponing tasks, is a common obstacle to effective time management. Understanding procrastination through the NLP lens can help identify underlying causes and provide solutions to overcome it.

Understanding Procrastination Through the NLP Lens

From an NLP perspective, procrastination isn't simply a bad habit or lack of discipline; it often indicates a conflict between different parts of our psyche. It might represent a mismatch between our conscious desires and unconscious fears or patterns. Understanding this can help target the root of the problem rather than just addressing the symptoms.

For instance, consciously, you might want to finish a report to meet a deadline, but unconsciously, you might associate completing the report with a fear of criticism or failure. Recognizing this conflict can be the first step towards resolving it and overcoming procrastination.

NLP Techniques to Overcome Procrastination

Parts Integration: This technique acknowledges that different parts of our psyche have different desires and motivations. It involves communicating with these parts to resolve conflicts and create internal harmony.

Example: You might want to finish a project (one part) but also want to avoid stress (another part). Through a dialogue between these parts, you could come to a solution like creating a balanced work schedule that allows you to progress on the project while also taking time for relaxation.

Swish Technique: This technique involves replacing an undesirable behavior (procrastination) with a desirable one (productive action). By visualizing the undesirable behavior and then 'swishing' it away and replacing it with the desirable behavior, you can begin to change your habits.

Example: Visualize yourself procrastinating, and then swiftly replace this image with a vivid image of yourself working productively. Repeat this until the productive image becomes your automatic response.

Anchoring: As discussed earlier, this technique involves creating a trigger or 'anchor' for a specific mental state. By creating an anchor for a state of productivity, you can help combat procrastination.

Example: You could use the act of opening your work document as an anchor. Over time, this action will become associated with starting work, which can help override the urge to procrastinate.

By understanding the root of procrastination and using NLP techniques to address it, you can make significant strides in improving your time management. These strategies aim to shift your mindset, change your habits, and promote a more productive and efficient use of time.

Chapter Nine: NLP for Stress Management and Work-Life Balance

Stress and an unbalanced work-life situation can significantly impact time management, causing distractions, hindering focus, and reducing productivity. NLP offers practical techniques to manage stress and improve work-life balance, ultimately enhancing time management.

The Impact of Stress on Time Management

Stress often leads to decreased efficiency and productivity. When we're stressed, our brain enters a state of hyperarousal, which can make focusing on tasks difficult and can lead to mistakes and oversights. Also, chronic stress can lead to burnout, further impacting our ability to manage time effectively.

For instance, if you're constantly worried about a personal issue, it can intrude on your work time, causing tasks to take longer than necessary or lead to procrastination. Thus, managing stress is crucial for effective time management.

Using NLP Techniques to Manage Stress and Improve Work-Life Balance

Dissociation: This NLP technique involves stepping outside of a stressful situation to see it from a different perspective. It can help create emotional distance, reducing the immediate stress response.

Example: If a work deadline is causing stress, imagine viewing the situation as an outside observer. This can help you see the situation more objectively and decrease stress levels.

Reframing: Reframing helps you change your interpretation of a situation, altering your emotional response. It can be useful for managing stress by helping you view stressors in a more positive or neutral light.

Example: If you're stressed about a large project, you could reframe it as an opportunity to showcase your skills and knowledge, changing the feeling of stress into a sense of challenge and motivation.

Self-Anchoring: This technique can be used to trigger a state of relaxation or calm. By associating a physical gesture or word with a calm state, you can use it to help manage stress.

Example: You could associate the action of deep breathing with a state of relaxation. Then, when you're feeling stressed, practicing deep breathing can help bring you back to a state of calm.

Work-Life Balance Visualization: Using NLP visualization techniques, you can imagine a balanced work-life situation and create a compelling vision of it. This can motivate you to take steps to make it a reality.

Example: Visualize your ideal day, where you have balanced your work tasks and personal activities effectively. By having a clear image of this balance, it can guide your actions and decisions.

By using NLP techniques to manage stress and improve work-life balance, you can remove significant barriers to effective time management. These techniques provide practical tools to navigate stressors, maintain focus, and achieve a more balanced and productive lifestyle.

In this chapter, we delve into **hypothetical case studies** and success stories, exploring how individuals and organizations have successfully applied NLP techniques to improve time management. These cases offer insights into the practical application and potential benefits of NLP in time management.

Examination of Individuals Who Have Successfully Applied NLP to Improve Time Management

Case Study 1: Jake, the Project Manager

Jake, a project manager, struggled with procrastination and often found himself working late hours to meet deadlines. He decided to use NLP techniques to address this issue.

He used the Parts Integration technique to reconcile the part of him that wanted to avoid stress with the part that wanted to meet his deadlines. Jake also started using the Swish technique, replacing images of himself procrastinating with images of productive work.

After several weeks of consistent practice, Jake noticed a significant reduction in procrastination. He was meeting his deadlines more comfortably and had more time for rest and recreation.

Case Study 2: Maria, the Entrepreneur

Maria, an entrepreneur, struggled with prioritizing tasks and often felt overwhelmed. She decided to try NLP techniques to improve her situation.

She used the Chunking technique to break down large tasks into manageable parts and the Outcome Specification technique to define what she wanted to achieve with each task. Maria also used the Meta-Modeling technique to clarify her goals and uncover potential obstacles.

After implementing these techniques, Maria found it easier to prioritize her tasks and felt less overwhelmed. Her time management improved, and she was able to focus more on strategic planning and business development.

Discussion on Organizations That Have Integrated NLP in Their Time Management Training Programs

Case Study 3: Tech Startup X

Tech Startup X found that their employees were struggling with time management, leading to missed deadlines and increasing stress levels. They decided to integrate NLP into their time management training program.

The training focused on NLP techniques like SMART Goal Setting, the Disney Strategy for decision making, and Anchoring for productivity. Employees were encouraged to visualize their tasks, set time-bound goals, and create productivity anchors.

After six months, the company noticed a marked improvement in project delivery times and employee stress levels. Employees reported feeling more in control of their time and more focused on their tasks.

Case Study 4: Marketing Agency Y

Marketing Agency Y found that high stress levels were impacting their employees' time management and work-life balance. They decided to introduce NLP techniques into their wellness and time management programs.

The programs taught employees how to use Dissociation and Reframing for stress management and Work-Life Balance Visualization to create a compelling vision of a balanced lifestyle.

After implementing these programs, the agency saw a decrease in staff turnover and an increase in productivity. Employees reported improved stress management and a better work-life balance, leading to better time management overall.

These hypothetical case studies highlight the potential of NLP techniques in improving time management at both individual and organizational levels. They offer real-world applications and demonstrate how incorporating NLP can lead to reduced stress, improved work-life balance, and enhanced productivity.

In this final chapter, we summarize the insights gathered throughout the book and look ahead to the potential future of NLP in time management and productivity. Moreover, we encourage readers to apply the knowledge and techniques discussed, promising transformative effects on their time management skills.

Summary of the Book's Insights

Throughout this book, we've delved into the intersections of Neuro-Linguistic Programming and time management. We've explored the fundamentals of NLP, its origins, core principles, and models, and the psychological aspects of time and the importance of managing it well.

We've examined how NLP can change our perception and utilization of time, utilizing techniques like anchoring and reframing. We've also delved into using NLP for setting and achieving SMART goals and for prioritizing tasks effectively.

We've discussed overcoming procrastination using NLP, highlighting techniques like parts integration and the swish technique. Furthermore, we've examined how NLP can be instrumental in stress management and maintaining a healthy work-life balance.

Through hypothetical case studies, we've illustrated how individuals and organizations can successfully apply NLP techniques to improve time management and productivity, reinforcing the practicality of these techniques in real-life scenarios.

The Potential Future of NLP in Time Management and Productivity

As our understanding of the human mind and its connection with behavior and time perception continues to evolve, the role of NLP in time management and productivity is expected to grow. NLP provides a framework for understanding and altering our mental processes, offering significant potential for enhancing personal and professional productivity.

With growing research in the field and increasing interest in personal development and productivity, we foresee a future where NLP techniques become commonplace in time management training programs, both at the individual and organizational levels.

Encouraging the Reader to Apply the Knowledge and Techniques Discussed

We encourage you, the reader, to apply the knowledge and techniques discussed in this book to your life. Remember, understanding the concepts is just the first step; the real transformation occurs when you consistently apply these techniques.

Whether it's setting SMART goals, managing stress, overcoming procrastination, or improving decision-making, these NLP techniques offer you a toolbox for improved time management.

By making these techniques a part of your daily life, you'll be able to transform your relationship with time, leading to improved productivity, reduced stress, and a more balanced and fulfilling life.

Thank you for embarking on this journey with us, and here's to your success in improving your time management skills using Neuro-Linguistic Programming!

Rex Morton is a renowned author and researcher in the United Kingdom with a passionate interest in the human mind, specifically in Cognitive Behavioural Therapy (CBT) and Neuro-Linguistic Programming (NLP).

Morton has spent a considerable portion of his professional life diving deep into the theories and principles that form the backbone of these two compelling fields. His fascination with NLP led him to complete an extensive certification program, solidifying his understanding of this innovative approach to understanding human behaviour.

Although Morton does not have clinical experience, his intense curiosity and dedication to studying these subjects have made him a respected figure in the field. He has thoroughly researched the integration of NLP techniques into CBT, offering fresh perspectives and insights into how these two methodologies can complement each other to enhance understanding of human cognition and behaviour.

As an author, Morton has successfully communicated his knowledge and passion to a broader audience, making complex psychological theories accessible to professionals and interested laypersons. His writing is characterized by a clear, engaging style and a focus on the practical application of theories, making them relevant to everyday life.

In his personal life, Morton is an ardent lover of the natural world, often spending his free time exploring the British countryside. His passion for landscape photography allows him to capture and share the beauty of these excursions. Despite his accomplishments, Morton is known for his humility and eagerness to continue learning. His work continues to inspire those interested in the intricate workings of the human mind and the exciting possibilities presented by the integration of NLP and CBT.

If you've found the content of this book enlightening and wish to continue your journey of understanding the human mind, I warmly invite you to visit my website at www.rexmorton.com. The website serves as a hub of knowledge where I share my latest findings, thoughts, and insights on the integration of NLP and CBT.

I also encourage you to subscribe to the newsletter available on the website. By subscribing, you'll receive regular updates on a range of topics, from detailed discussions on specific NLP techniques and their application in CBT, to the latest research in the field.

The newsletter is also the first place I'll share news of upcoming releases. Whether it's the announcement of a new book, the launch of an online course, newsletter subscribers will be the first to know. This is a great opportunity to continue learning directly from me, deepening your understanding of NLP and CBT, and enhancing your skills in applying these techniques in your own life or professional practice.

I'm looking forward to sharing this journey with you.

www.ingramcontent.com/pod-product-compliance
Lightning Source LLC
Chambersburg PA
CBHW060853260726
48661CB00008B/3243